The Dragon who Grew

Also by Joan Cass

THE WITCH OF WITCHERY WOOD
THE WITCH AND THE NAUGHTY PRINCESSES
THE WITCHES' LOST SPELL BOOK
TROUBLE AMONG THE WITCHES
THE WITCHES' SCHOOL

The Dragon who Grew

and other stories

JOAN CASS

Illustrated by Steve Smallman

from

Joan E. Cass

with Good wishes

HODDER AND STOUGHTON
LONDON SYDNEY AUCKLAND TORONTO

British Library Cataloguing in Publication Data

Cass, Joan
    The dragon who grew and other stories.
    I. Title   II. Smallman, Steve
    823'.914[J]   PZ7

    ISBN 0-340-39356-4

Published by Hodder and Stoughton Children's Books,
a division of Hodder and Stoughton Ltd,
Mill Road, Dunton Green, Sevenoaks, Kent TN13 2YJ

Photoset by Rowland Phototypesetting Ltd,
Bury St Edmunds, Suffolk

Printed in Great Britain by
T. J. Press (Padstow) Ltd,
Padstow, Cornwall

To Romney and Tarragon
with much love

Contents

Take Care

When you approach a dragon, try
To look him firmly in the eye.
Be sure he's gentle, brave and kind
And has no evil plan in mind.
Do not offend, and be polite,
Cause no anxiety or fright.
Inquire about his health and note
If he is blowing too much smoke
In an unpleasant smoky style,
In case he is about to eat
You casually from head to feet.
If so, it would be wise to say,
'I'm wishing you a happy day,'
And very quietly steal away!

The Dragon who Grew

Ah Ming was a dragon. A very large dragon. When he breathed it looked rather as if he had a great, hot fire inside him because he puffed out so much smoke. His tail seemed to stretch for miles and miles.

He had not always been so large and imposing, for when he was only a few years old he was very small and thin with no tail at all. In fact, his mother, who was a beautiful size and shape, was quite ashamed of him.

'I do wish Ah Ming would grow a little,' she said to the other dragons. 'No one will ever be frightened of him.'

This made Ah Ming very unhappy, and tears would run down his dragon cheeks. He decided to run away.

'I will find a new home,' he said, 'where I can live happily all by myself.'

So one dark night, when a tiny moon gave just enough light for Ah Ming to see the road, he left home. He felt a little sad and lonely leaving all the other dragons, but he was quite determined to make his own way in the world.

He was so small that he was able to take the little paths and tracks which wound between the hills, and by morning he had gone quite a long way. He slept in the sun under a tree and waited until it was dark before moving on again. He travelled like this for several days.

One morning he came to a place where tall trees grew on the top of a hill. There was a huge rocky cave out of which a stream bubbled, and down below in the valley he could see a village. It was a lovely, quiet place.

'I shall stay here for ever and ever and ever,' said Ah Ming happily.

So he settled down and ate wild fruits and the little mushrooms that sprang up on the hillside, and drank the cold water from the little stream.

Weeks and weeks went by. From the grassy mound outside his cave Ah Ming had a wonderful view of the village below him in the valley. He watched the children playing, everyone going shopping, and the carts and wagons moving along the road.

One bright, sunny morning Ah Ming decided he would go down to the village and make friends with everyone, for he felt sure they would like him. I am such a tiny, gentle, kind dragon, he thought, even the little children will want to play with me.

So, when the sun was high in the sky and the street full of noise and bustle, Ah Ming suddenly appeared. He expected everyone to come running to greet him, but instead there was the most terrible confusion. People dropped everything and ran; doors were slammed; and mothers hid their children. In a moment the street was empty.

'Oh dear, oh dear, whatever is the matter?' said Ah Ming. 'Surely they can't be frightened of me!'

He walked very slowly and carefully down the village street until he came to a fountain in a lovely clear pool of water. Sitting on the low wall round the pool was a small boy. Ah Ming stopped at once and he and the boy looked at each other.

'Why has everybody run away but you?' said Ah Ming. 'I'm just a small, kind, gentle dragon.'

'Really?' said the little boy in surprise. 'I'm afraid everyone was very, very frightened of you. I nearly ran away myself but my grandfather had told me such wonderful tales about dragons, I thought I would stay and see what you looked like. How very, very large you are.'

'Large!' said Ah Ming in astonishment. 'Me! I'm almost the smallest dragon in the world.'

'You've made a big mistake,' said the boy. 'Just look at yourself.'

Ah Ming turned and looked down into the bright, clear water of the pool and saw his

14

reflection. He was simply enormous. He was
puffing out clouds of smoke, his neck curved
high, his tail stretched out behind him. 'Oh
dear, oh dear,' said Ah Ming. 'What has
happened to me?'

'You've grown,' said the small boy, 'that's
all, but you look simply beautiful, a real

dragon. As long as you don't eat people, I will hurry off and tell everyone you are quite harmless.'

In a short time Ah Ming was surrounded by an admiring crowd. Children climbed on his back and little boys slid down his tail. He felt very happy. Everybody liked him. After a lot of talk, the Village Council decided that they wanted to adopt Ah Ming as their special dragon.

Every day he came down from his cave and stretched out in the village street. He took up a great deal of room but he looked magnificent, and the children loved playing with him.

He felt very satisfied and contented. Luckily, he stopped growing.

Chang and the Robbers

Chang, the youngest and smallest of three dragon children, was kind and gentle, but he was always asking questions. He wanted to know what was happening everywhere in the world. This pleased his parents, who felt Chang would grow up to be a wise and clever dragon, but his brother and sister got a little tired of him. 'Oh, go and blow smoke-rings,' they would say. 'Leave us in peace.'

So Chang blew smoke-rings all by himself until he could make beautiful curling shapes and patterns.

One evening, after supper, the dragon family were lying quietly in front of their cave on the top of the hill. Chang was in one of his 'I'm going to ask questions' moods.

'What lies beyond those far-distant mountains?' he asked.

'A new and exciting world,' said his father.

'And where does the spring come from that bubbles out of our cave?' asked Chang.

'From inside the mountain, I expect,' said his mother, 'for there are many strange, dark, underground passages we are far too large to explore.'

'Chang might be able to get through if he went without his meals for a few weeks,' said his sister.

'Yes, go and lose yourself there,' said his brother, for although neither of them wanted to be unkind, they were playing snap-dragon and hated being disturbed.

Chang thought this a very exciting idea, so he ate very small meals for the next day or two, and tried to get thin. Then, one night, when the family had settled down quietly to sleep, he made his way to the back of the cave where the stream bubbled out from its dark hole. The water was very cold but not too deep and Chang splashed happily along. The stream twisted and turned between high rock walls and then suddenly vanished. On his left, however, was a dark, narrow passage; perhaps it led to the village.

Chang started off. The path went on and on for a long way downhill, and then suddenly it ended in front of a huge door. Chang gave it a push, it swung back, and he found himself in a large room full of chests and cupboards, and piles of books and papers. He realised that he must be in the vault of the village bank where everyone kept their most treasured possessions.

Chang felt a little weary, so he lay down quietly on the floor to get his breath. The ceiling above him was made of wooden planks but they didn't fit very closely together. Suddenly, he heard low voices from overhead. Who could possibly be in the bank at midnight?

A husky voice said, 'Now, have you got all the duplicate keys and the tools to open the chests and cupboards? Remember they are full of treasures.'

'We'll put them in these sacks,' said a second voice. 'Then we'll carry them through the dark streets to our boat which lies by the jetty. Before sunrise we shall be miles away down the river.'

Chang was horrified. He looked up at the wooden ceiling – and then he had an idea! If he started puffing out smoke-rings, they would slowly seep through the gaps in the wooden planks and the robbers would think the bank was on fire.

Chang took a few slow, deep breaths and then started puffing out magnificent smoke-rings into the room above.

'Whatever is happening?' said a voice. 'The bank's on fire! Hurry, hurry, get some water!' There was a terrific scurrying and commotion up above, for the room was becoming most uncomfortable, and the robbers were scared out of their wits. 'Let's get out before we are burned to death!' they yelled.

The smoke was drifting through the windows into the street where a late-night

traveller saw it. 'The bank's on fire, the bank's on fire!' he shouted. Windows were thrown open and people put out their heads.

Meanwhile, the robbers made their escape as fast as they could, running towards the river where their boat was moored.

The bank doors had been left half-open by the fleeing robbers; some of the villagers hurried inside, while others brought buckets of water to put out the fire.

Chang stopped blowing smoke-rings and, when the door to the vault was opened, he was sitting quietly on the floor looking a little tired but otherwise quite calm and collected.

'Chang, where have you come from and what has happened?' Everyone started asking Chang questions. He explained how he had discovered the passage which led to the bank vault and had heard the robbers planning to steal all the treasures of the village.

Everyone praised and congratulated Chang on his brave and clever behaviour, and his wonderful smoke-rings, until he glowed with pleasure. Then he thought he had better go home the way he had come, through the long underground passage, back to his family. Everyone was still asleep when at last he got back.

Chang's father and mother were very proud when they heard of his adventures, but his brother and sister were a little annoyed.

'We can't think why you have such exciting adventures and we don't,' they grumbled.

'Never mind,' said Chang. 'It will be your turn next.'

The Dragon that was Too Hot

Sun Ling was a very large, long, green and black dragon with eyes that shone like rubies. He had a very beautiful dragon wife called Sing Koo and three fine dragon children.

They lived on the top of a little hill in a huge cave out of which a stream bubbled. It was a quiet, restful place. There were tall pine trees growing nearby, providing shade from the hot sun, and there was green grass to lie on.

Down below in the valley there was a little village which Sun Ling knew very well. He often went there, for the villagers were his friends and were always glad to see him.

He would make his way slowly and carefully down the village street, between the stalls and the crowds of bustling people, and the children would get on his back and feed him with sweets and cakes.

Sometimes when he went visiting Sun Ling took his beautiful wife, Sing Koo, and his three dragon children with him. Everyone in the village would come out to welcome them for they were kind, thoughtful dragons who never did anyone any harm.

However, Tang Soo, the youngest dragon, was only allowed to go if he stayed outside the village and kept away from everybody. This was because poor Tang Soo suffered from a terrible dragon complaint. When he breathed he puffed out so much hot, fiery smoke he burnt the grass all round him, turned the water in the village fountain into clouds of steam, and singed the clothes of the children who came too near. He was, in fact, a very, very, hot fiery dragon.

This upset Tang Soo very much for he was very gentle and friendly. He loved company, especially the company of children.

'You will grow out of it,' said his mother, Sing Koo, kindly. 'But I'm afraid it may take a long time.'

Every night, even though it was most uncomfortable, Tang Soo slept in the spring of
water that flowed through the cave in which
they all lived. The water was bitterly cold.

Perhaps, thought Tang Soo as he shed a
few hot dragon tears, the cold, cold water
from the spring will cool me, and in the
morning when I wake I shall be better and
just like other dragons. When morning came,

26

however, Tang Soo was always just the same. His brother and sister tried to comfort him, but he could not help feeling lonely and unwanted.

Spring, summer and autumn passed and the dragon family lived very happily together. Then winter arrived with freezing winds and icy snow. There had never been such a terrible winter. The path down the hillside to the village was steep and slippery and Sun Ling and Sing Koo and their dragon children stayed in their cave where it was warm and sheltered.

One icy morning, when Sun Ling went to the cave's entrance to see what the weather was like, he saw three people from the village struggling up the steep hill-path towards him. They were the village elders, all wearing their thickest padded clothes. When they saw Sun Ling they hurried towards him as fast as they could over the thick snow.

'We have come on a very important mission,' said the oldest of the village elders, bowing to Sun Ling. 'Down in our village the snow lies thick and heavy. The water in the fountain is frozen, and icicles are hanging from the roofs of the houses. The snow is so deep in the streets we cannot get about and do our work. It lies in huge drifts, heaped against our doors. We do not know what to do for we have never had a winter like this before. We have come to ask if we might borrow your son, Tang Soo. Perhaps if he came down to the village and puffed out clouds of hot, fiery smoke and walked slowly up and down the village street, the ice and snow would melt.'

Tang Soo was delighted when he heard this. At last he could be of some use to the people in the village he liked so much. He hurried down the hill in front of the village elders, leaving a wet trail in the snow behind him.

Arriving in the village he at once began to walk very, very slowly down the village street, puffing out enormous clouds of hot, fiery smoke. When he got to the end of the

street he turned round and came very, very
slowly back.

The snow began to melt like magic. The
icicles fell from the eaves of the houses, the
snow slid from the roofs. The frozen fountain
began to bubble with water. People opened
their doors and windows and shouted to each
other with excitement.

Then Tang Soo made his way very, very carefully through all the tiny lanes and by-ways of the village, into the courtyards, down winding steps, through gateways, then down across the fields to the river. It took quite a long time.

All the while Tang Soo breathed and breathed in great, huge gasps. He was so enveloped in hot, fiery smoke he could scarcely be seen. At last, however, there was no ice and snow left. People came out of their houses, shops were opened again and stalls set up. The children began to laugh and play.

By the time Tang Soo got back to the village he felt very, very tired but very proud and happy too. He found he could not move another step so he lay down in the middle of the village street, among the stalls and the people, and went to sleep.

When he woke the sun was shining in the sky and everyone was going about their business. The children playing in the street gathered round him with sweet spicy cakes.

Then Tang Soo suddenly discovered that when he breathed he only puffed out pleasant, warm smoke. The children were no longer nearly scorched when they came near him. In fact, they could safely sit on his neck or play with his tail without getting burnt. He was cured!

Tang Soo was simply delighted. 'How wonderful,' he said. 'Now I am an ordinary dragon just like the rest of my family. I must hurry home to tell them the good news.'

Everyone in the village was grateful to Tang Soo. The Town Council presented him with a beautiful necklace of beads and the children tied a green banner on his tail, which said: THANK YOU TANG SOO, and Tang Soo was the happiest dragon in the world.

Tung Wing, the Unlucky Dragon

Tung Wing was a very unlucky dragon. If things went wrong, they always went wrong for him.

His parents would say, 'Be careful, Tung Wing. Look where you are going, Tung Wing. Don't fall over those rocks, Tung Wing. Don't make yourself so conspicious, Tung Wing.' The result was he forgot to be careful, didn't look where he was going, was always falling over rocks and calling attention to himself.

One morning Tung Wing and some of his friends were playing down on a large grassy meadow just below their home among the mountains. A wide road ran across the meadow, and sometimes large caravans went by, or perhaps small groups of folk travelling on to the next village with their carts, taking vegetables and fruit to sell at the near-by markets.

Most of the people who travelled the road were the dragons' friends but occasionally a caravan of strange, fierce-looking men would pass, men who shouted and cursed, had large whips in their hands and seemed ready to attack any one who got in their way. Then the dragons would quickly hide in the long grass or behind the thick bushes, so that the strange, frightening men would not see them.

One day, however, when they were happily playing, they heard the shouts of men and women and a huge cavalcade appeared. There were wagons and carts, horses and ponies and elephants, and lots of noisy, shouting children running everywhere. The dragons, as usual, had hidden themselves very quickly and carefully, well away from the road and the inquisitive children – all except for Tung Wing, of course.

He was a small dragon but he was also very curious and, in spite of all the warnings his parents had given him, he could not resist poking his head above the long grass to see what was happening. Of course, the children who were running wild and shouting and singing saw his head poking above the grass and called to their parents.

Soon Tung Wing found himself surrounded by a crowd of strange, curious people who pinched and prodded him. He didn't like it at all.

'Just what we need for our side-show, a curious beast,' said a tall man with a red handkerchief tied round his head and a whip in his hand. He picked up Tung Wing by his long tail and swung him over his shoulder.

'Never seen anything like this before,' he laughed. 'Just the sort of sensation we need at the circus, something different, and we have got an empty cage as well.'

He carried Tung Wing off over his shoulder and everyone walked back to the road. Tung Wing found himself heaved into a small dirty cage lashed to the back of one of

the wagons. Then he heard the roar of lions and he knew he must have been captured for a Chinese travelling circus. He was terrified. It was hot and stuffy in the cage, for it was very small and dirty.

As it got dark the cavalcade of wagons, carts and caged animals arrived at the little Chinese town, and in a large field they began to unpack. A huge tent was erected, cages of wild animals were set up, and stalls and side-shows appeared.

Still in his tiny cage, Tung Wing found himself raised up in full view of the public, who crowded round to look at him. His tail was pulled, he was prodded and pinched. People thrust bits of food through the bars of the cage but Tung Wing was not hungry. It was hot and stuffy. He was tired, thirsty and miserable.

A day or two went by. Tung Wing felt very ill and so unhappy that he thought he was going to die. No one seemed to bother about his comfort and the cage was so small he could hardly stretch his legs and his long tail.

Now, amongst the circus children there was one little dark-haired girl who was kind to him. She brought him food and fresh water and spoke to him gently.

'Poor little dragon,' she said, 'I know you are a dragon even if no one else does. In the little village where I once lived, before my family joined the circus, there were several kindly dragons who came down to see us and I remember them well. I was so happy living in the village with my parents and two brothers. Then we were persuaded to join the circus and we have all been so miserable. I want to help you if I can.'

The time came for the circus to move on to the next little town. But that evening, when it was dark and everyone had gone to bed, the little girl crept out with the key of Tung Wing's cage in her hand.

'Little dragon,' she said, 'I'm going to set you free, then I shall fetch my own faithful pony and I shall take you back to the green meadow where your friends play and your family live. It is a long journey, but we shall ride all night.'

The little girl unlocked the cage, and Tung Wing clung on to her on the back of her pony as they galloped through the night, back along the road to the green meadow and the

mountains where Tung Wing's family dwelt. As the sun rose, Tung Wing saw that he was nearly home.

The little girl dismounted from her pony to help Tung Wing to the ground. Then she turned and, with a wave of her hand, she galloped off back to the circus and vanished in the distance.

Tung Wing was so stiff and tired that he could hardly walk, but he struggled slowly across the grass and began to climb the mountain path. Then, suddenly, he saw his parents and friends and he knew, he knew he was safely back home.

Everyone was overjoyed at his return, for they had thought they would never see him again. A wonderful meal was prepared, a soft bed was made up, and Tung Wing had never felt so happy and so wanted before.

He spent the day telling everyone about his adventures and all the things that had happened to him. And the very next day the dragons were visited by the little girl and her parents, who had decided to leave the circus and return to their own village.

The adventure taught Tung Wing a lesson. In future he tried to be more sensible, to look where he was going, and to avoid boastful escapades. And, most important of all, he learned to listen to his parents.

The Small Dragons to the Rescue

On a broad plateau up in the mountains, where tall trees grew thick and dense and a little stream of clear water poured down the mountain-side, there lived two groups of dragons in their own special caves – the large dragons and the small dragons.

Alas, they were not on speaking terms. The large dragons despised the small dragons, whom they said were puny little things; while the small dragons disliked the large dragons because they said they were so fat and clumsy. So, instead of getting on with each other, they either didn't speak at all, or they grumbled and complained all the time.

The young dragons in both groups liked to play together, but when their parents discovered this they were parted at once.

'I can't think why we are not allowed to

play together,' grumbled the children of the large dragons. 'Because,' said their parents, 'small dragons are not to be trusted and will get you into trouble.'

'Nonsense,' said the children of the large dragons. 'We like them and we can get into trouble without *their* help.'

The small dragons were told by their parents that the children of the large dragons were greedy and lazy.

'But so are we,' moaned the small dragons.

Things went on like this until one day something happened. A baby dragon from the family of the large dragons fell down into a deep hole in the mountain and, as he fell, he brought down a cascade of earth and small rocks which almost buried him.

This wouldn't have happened if he had looked where he was going, but he was a very careless little dragon. Of course, he couldn't get out. The sides of the hole were too steep and slippery, and his parents were too large and heavy to climb down to rescue him.

The Small Dragons to the Rescue

So, there he was, looking up into the sunlight and wondering what he could possibly do, and crying large dragon tears.

Meanwhile, both groups of dragons had heard what had happened and they gathered round to see. The large dragons had to keep well away from the edge of the hole in case it caved in. Then the poor baby dragon would have been buried alive and smothered.

Now the small dragons were kindly creatures at heart and would help anyone in difficulty, even a large dragon.

'Well, you know what I think,' said one of the small dragons. 'We could form a dragon chain down into the hole if we all held on to each other's tails. Then the baby dragon could grasp the last tail and we could slowly pull him to safety. We are strong but we are very light on our feet because we are small and agile. We shall be *very* careful.'

So that was what they did. They formed the dragon chain, and the baby dragon found he was able to catch hold of the last dragon's tail

and hold on tight. Then the dragon chain
moved very, very slowly and the baby dragon
was pulled safely into the sunlight as his
parents watched anxiously, hoping nothing

dreadful would happen. They were still a little suspicious of the small dragons.

Everything went according to plan. The baby dragon, his tears dried, was reunited with his family, the large dragons were overcome with gratitude, and there was great rejoicing.

Down in the little Chinese village at the foot of the mountain the villagers could see both groups of dragons talking to each other, and appearing very happy and pleased.

'Something has happened,' they murmured. 'Those two groups of dragons are actually on speaking terms at last – and high time too.'

Soon the villagers heard exactly what had happened as both groups of dragons were anxious to tell everyone how they were now all friends. All the dragons hurried down the mountainside to the village inn, which sold delicious spicy cakes. They took up a great deal of room crowding round the tables, and they ate as many spicy cakes as the villagers could produce, but nobody minded. Living near such quarrelsome dragons had been really unpleasant. But now all was well, the quarrels were over, and the dragons remained friends for the rest of their lives.

Wat Yin defeats the Robbers

Wat Yin was a strange dragon. Instead of living in a pleasant, dry cave on a mountain plateau, with other friendly dragons near-by, he decided to live on a damp, soggy patch of ground near a small lake. There were groups of willow trees, short springy grass, tall rushes, a rather pebbly little beach and a small jetty.

People from the nearby Chinese village used to come down to fish in the lake or row across to the other side where there were some very small sandy beaches. The village children, too, used to come down in the summer to sit on the jetty and fish.

Wat Yin was quite a useful dragon in that he generally kept an eye on the children when they were playing near the water, and the villagers knew he would rescue them if any of them was foolish enough to fall in.

Naturally, however, he often dozed off in the sun, lying among the willow trees by the lake-shore, and sometimes he went for a swim among the water lilies.

In many ways it was an attractive little lake, especially in summer, but in the winter it was damp and cold. It rained, the wind was bitter, and Wat Yin got rheumatism. He was very obstinate, though, and nothing would make him move. One day he was lying curled up among the willows, quite out of sight, idly watching what was going on. There were two boys fishing, but everyone else was busy in the fields.

Then, in the distance, Wat Yin suddenly heard the sound of voices, and coming towards the shore he saw a small boat rowed by several very unpleasant and uncouth-looking men. He realised they were robbers who stole goods from the villagers, destroyed their crops, and took their children who, of course, were never seen again.

48

Wat Yin defeats the Robbers

Wat Yin heard their voices over the water. 'Two likely-looking boys over by the jetty,' shouted one of the robbers. 'Just what we need, two boys to cook and clean for us. We'll pick them up.'

Wat Yin wondered what to do. Should he emerge from the willows and frighten away the robbers, or stay where he was? After all, he thought to himself, the lads must learn to take care of themselves. They knew the dangers, they were young and quick . . . He closed his eyes.

Then, suddenly, he heard cries for help and saw the two boys being dragged by the robbers on to their boat. In a moment it set off, taking the lads across the lake.

Wat Yin felt very guilty. He should have gone to their help instead of doing nothing. Now what was he going to do? It was getting dark. The boys would not be missed. Sometimes they stayed the night with friends or slept in a little hut by the lake-side.

Across the water he could see the dim lights

of the robbers' headquarters, a large boat moored by the bank where a narrow outlet led beyond the lake into the river. By morning they could be miles away.

He realised he must go to their rescue. Very slowly and carefully he slipped into the water and swam swiftly but silently across the lake, to where the robbers' boat was moored. Through the portholes he could see the robbers drinking and playing cards. The two boys were lying on the deck, tied up with rope.

The boys saw him and Wat Yin managed to rear up in the water and pull them towards him. Then, with his sharp teeth, he bit through the ropes that bound them and they were free.

'Now climb on to my back,' Wat Yin instructed the boys. Of course, all this made a lot of splashing noise and the robbers saw them.

'What's that,' they shouted. 'A horrible monster!' Wat Yin started to blow out clouds

of hot, fiery smoke, his eyes glowed red, and he looked very, very alarming.

The robbers were terrified. 'Leave the creature alone,' they shouted to each other. 'He will sink us or set us on fire. Let him go; frighten him away.'

Enveloped in fiery smoke, Wat Yin swam towards the other shore with the two boys clinging to his neck, leaving the cries of the robbers far behind.

'Oh, thank you, thank you, dear brave dragon,' they cried. 'We were so scared. We thought we would never see our homes again. Please don't tell our parents. They will be very angry with us for not being more careful, as they have warned us about the robbers.'

At last they reached the shore and the boys, wet and cold, hurried off home. Wat Yin went back to his sheltered spot among the willow trees and curled up ready to go to sleep. He felt very satisfied with his efforts, for he knew he had done the right thing. And, in spite of the damp in winter and his rheumatism, he felt he had to stay for ever by the lake, guarding the villagers from harm.

Meanwhile, the robbers got ready to leave the district. They were determined that they would never, ever, return to raid the village.

The Lost Dragon
who found his Way Home

Su See was a lonely little dragon. He could not remember exactly what had happened to him but he knew that he had once had parents and brothers and sisters. He remembered, too, that there had been a terrible storm. Rain had poured down, trees crashed to the ground, mountain streams had become raging torrents and somehow he had got separated from his family and was swept away by the swift-flowing flood.

He had finally managed to struggle out of the water and crouched, exhausted and shivering with cold, on a little rock by the rushing mountain stream. There he had been found by a kindly group of dragons who had taken Su See home with them to their own retreat in the mountains.

The storm had gradually abated but Su See

was now miles away from his home and his family. He tried to describe the mountains where he had lived, but no one seemed to have heard of them. He felt very unhappy, for he missed his home and his family and, although the other dragons were kind to him, he tended to wander off by himself.

Sometimes he joined one or two of the younger dragons when they went down to the little Chinese village where the villagers were always very kind and friendly to them.

One day he was sitting alone in the village street, feeling particularly miserable, with large tears running down his little dragon cheeks. Suddenly he heard a voice speaking to him and he looked up and saw a little boy who had sat down beside him.

'Little dragon,' said the boy, 'what has happened to make you cry so bitterly?'

So Su See told the little boy all his troubles and how much he missed his home and his family.

'You are like me,' said the little boy. 'I was

54

found huddled under some trees after that terrible storm. I, too, have been separated from my family and although I am well cared for by the village folk I miss my parents and my brothers and sisters and long to see them again.'

Now that Su See had found a friend in the village he often went down to meet him, and together they talked about their homes, their parents and their brothers and sisters.

'I think,' said the little boy one day when he and Su See were talking together, 'now that the warm weather is here and the days are bright and sunny, you and I will travel together. We will cross the valley and follow the stream that runs down the mountain-side. Somewhere in those mountains there is a little valley where I am sure my parents live, and among the caves and rocks and trees I am sure you will find your family and your brothers and sisters, for I remember clearly that dragons used to live there.'

So, early one morning, Su See and the little

boy set off on their travels. It was a weary-some journey. The mountains were high and steep as they followed the little stream upward. There were forest paths to negotiate, and at night they found shelter under the trees that grew near the stream.

The little boy had brought a bag of food with him, and they gathered wild fruits and berries. Sometimes they caught fish in the pools in the stream, and lit a little fire and cooked them. Then one morning as the sun rose the little boy gave a shout.

'Look,' he said. 'There on that little plateau on the mountain slope I can see a village, with people moving about. I'm sure that is where I lived. Let us hurry and see.'

The little boy was right. As they got nearer to the village he recognised people he knew and suddenly he saw his parents and his brothers and sisters.

There was a wonderful reunion and everyone was delighted to see him again.

Su See felt very sad. He was happy that the little boy was united with his family again, but he was more lonely than ever. He wandered up a narrow path and suddenly, to his joy, he saw some caves and a small group of dragons who looked familiar.

Could they be his very own family? He had been parted from them so long ago that he wasn't sure. His brothers and sisters had grown up since then; and they might not recognise him either. Then a large motherly-looking dragon came down the path to meet him.

'Su See,' cried his mother. 'You've come home.'

And Su See was the happiest little dragon in the whole of China.

In Search of Dragons

Wen Peng was a little Chinese boy who lived in a small village on a wide plain. It was a pleasant place to live, and Wen Peng went to the village school.

Every Friday afternoon one of the elders of the village used to come and tell the children stories. Wen Peng loved listening to the stories, especially those about dragons, and he wanted to see a real dragon more than anything else in the world.

'Aren't there any dragons left in China any more?' Wen Peng kept asking the old storyteller.

'No, I am afraid they have all vanished,' said Cho Kuan sadly.

Wen Peng just could not believe this. He dreamt about dragons, he drew pictures of dragons and he made up his mind to go on a

59

long pilgrimage when he was a little older, and find out for himself if, somewhere in China, there were dragons still living.

He waited and planned and thought about dragons. Then one morning he packed a bag to carry over his shoulder with food and a few clothes, said goodbye to his friends, and set off on his travels to find the dragons he was sure still lived somewhere in China. After climbing up a steep mountain path he descended into a valley where a small village nestled. He was welcomed enthusiastically by the village folk.

'Please, Wen Peng,' they said, 'stay a little while. The teacher in our village school is ill and there is no one to educate our children.' So Wen Peng stayed and taught the village children for a few weeks.

Then, one morning when the sun had just risen, he started off on his travels again. He crossed wide green plains and low mountains dotted with trees. He saw rocks piled up, looking as if they would touch the sky. He crossed little streams of water running across flat fields. In the rivers the villagers were catching fish. In the fields they were sowing rice. Sometimes the sun shone and it was hot and Wen Peng sat and ate his food in the shade of trees. Sometimes, in the foothills of the mountains, snow was lying and bitter winds blew.

Sometimes he came to Chinese towns full of hurrying people. There were stalls laden with fruit and vegetables and shops selling all sorts of exciting things. Everywhere he went he asked the people if they knew anything about dragons. Had they seen any? If so, where did they live?

Alas, the people only laughed kindly at him and said there were no longer any dragons left alive.

Once, at one of the Chinese festivals in a busy little town, he saw a wonderful procession with huge dragons among the crowds. They looked beautiful, and Wen Peng was very excited. Alas, he found they were not

real dragons at all, but were all made of
gaily-painted paper and cardboard. So he left
the towns and the big villages behind him and
walked, and walked, until he found himself
among low mountain peaks with little green
valleys and tiny Chinese villages nestling in

the hollows at the foot of the hills.

The village folk there were very kind, and when he asked them about dragons they didn't laugh at him at all.

'Oh yes,' they said, 'we have dragons living near-by, among the caves in the low hills. You can see them quite easily. They are very friendly and kind and understand our speech. We are very fond of them. They visit us, and if you climb up the mountain paths you will find them sleeping and playing among the rocks in the little valley.'

Wen Peng was delighted, and the next morning he was up at sunrise. He took a little path which led him up the mountain-side where he could look down on one of the little green valleys.

There in the sunshine he saw the dragons. The morning light caught the colours of their glistening scales: gold, green, orange and red. They were even more magnificent than Wen Pen had imagined them to be.

It did not take Wen Peng long to make

friends with the dragons as they often came down to the villages and helped the villagers in all sorts of ways.

Wen Peng was happy at last. Now he *knew* that there were still dragons alive in China, and he decided to stay with his beloved dragons for the rest of his life.

Cho Kuan, the Greedy Dragon

Cho Kuan was a large, very fat dragon. He was not at all popular, however, with the other dragons with whom he lived on a hill overlooking a little Chinese village. He was so very greedy.

If he found a lovely bed of wild strawberries he ate them all himself and never told anyone!

If he found a deserted orchard with the ground covered with fallen apples he ate them all himself and never told anyone!

If he found a field covered with tasty young mushrooms he ate them all himself and never told anyone!

The spot where the dragons lived was a little plateau among the mountains, with narrow paths and cool dark caves. Below, in the valley, they could see the small Chinese village and the villagers who were friendly and welcoming.

Now Cho Kuan had to live in a very large cave with a huge entrance because he was so fat.

'Some day,' said one of the dragons, 'Cho Kuan will squeeze in through his doorway and he won't be able to squeeze out. He keeps a very large store of food in there and eats it in the night when he gets hungry. He'll grow so fat he won't be able to move.'

'That would be most unfortunate,' murmured the other dragons, but it was no use warning Cho Kuan – he didn't listen to anyone.

It was Cho Kuan's birthday and the other dragons planned a lovely party for him with all sorts of special dragon delicacies. Cho Kuan ate and ate, as much as he could, and as usual he was so greedy he devoured more food than any of the other dragons. When he went to bed that night he could only just squeeze through the door of his cave.

Cho Kuan, the Greedy Dragon

As a rule the weather in the mountains where the dragons lived was pleasantly fine and warm, but on the night of Cho Kuan's party it suddenly and unexpectedly changed. There was a terrible storm. The wind blew, the snow fell. In the morning all the little paths to the plateau where the dragons lived were blocked with fallen trees and rocks and deep, dangerous snow drifts. The dragons were marooned and could not even get down to the village.

For a while, all went well. The dragons were safe and warm in their caves, and there was plenty of food stored away. After a time, however, the food began to run out. Eventually, Cho Kuan was the only dragon who had anything left to eat as all the crevices in his cave were filled with a variety of delicious edibles. One morning, he was awakened by sounds of crying outside the door of his cave, and when he put his head out he saw four baby dragons sitting there.

'Oh please, Cho Kuan,' they said as tears

ran down their little dragon cheeks, 'could you give us something to eat from your store of food? We are so hungry. We have had no supper and no breakfast.'

Cho Kuan was very annoyed. 'There is only enough for myself,' he said angrily. 'Don't worry me,' and he withdrew into his cave. As the day passed, however, he couldn't forget the four baby dragons. He kept seeing their little faces with large tears running down their cheeks and hearing their sobs. Suppose they all died and all the other dragons went away and left him all alone. What would he do? Finally he put his head out of his cave. It was very quiet, but he could still hear the baby dragons crying. Cho Kuan helped himself to a large plateful of food from his store – and he found he couldn't eat it.

Then, as the day passed, he felt more and more miserable. Finally he could bear it no longer so he squeezed himself slowly through his door to see what was happening. The dragons were wandering about in the snow,

looking depressed and miserable, and trying to comfort the baby dragons, who were still crying. They were all very hungry.

'I've come to tell you,' said Cho Kuan rather reluctantly, 'I've still got plenty of provisions left and I'd like to share them with you.'

The dragons were speechless with astonishment. Cho Kuan went into his cave and came out with dishes of appetising food. Soon all the dragons were sitting down to a sumptuous meal, and the baby dragons had dried their tears.

The food just lasted out. As the dragons were finishing their final meal, the sun suddenly appeared, the snow melted, soft rain fell, the grass began to grow and the leaves of the trees unfurled. The famine was over!

In the meantime, although Cho Kuan had not noticed it, he had grown very slim. He found he could move about quite easily and had lots of energy. He became very popular and the baby dragons adored him, especially when he started telling them bedtime stories.

Every now and then, of course, Cho Kuan finds himself longing to eat a very large meal all by himself but he resists the temptation and he has never really regretted it. He is now slim, kindly and generous, and much loved by all the dragons.

The Treasure in the Mountains

Tucked away between tall mountain peaks, high above the plains below, was a little Chinese village. There was a long road which wound downhill to the wide plain where the small towns were clustered.

In the summer it was hot and damp but the villagers were able to grow fruit and vegetables which they sold in the markets in the nearby towns.

In the winter it was very cold. Snow covered the mountains and bitter winds blew. The villagers put on their warmest clothes and the smoke from their wood-fires rose into the sky above.

In spite of the weather, and the fact that everyone had to work hard, the villagers were very contented. They had a pleasant Village School, a Town Hall, and a fine Market Place.

There was, however, one serious thing that troubled them.

The mountains were full of dark caves and long, narrow passages. It was easy to get lost and no one liked to venture in alone. But there had always been rumours that huge amounts of treasure lay hidden in the caves; stories of rich kings and princes fleeing from their kingdoms to the safety of the mountains, bringing their treasures with them, and tales of pirates from the near-by sea-port who hid their bags of gold in the holes and crannies in the caves.

The villagers were constantly being harassed by bands of robbers who had heard of the treasures, and threatened them, saying, 'We will destroy your crops and steal your children if you do not tell us where this treasure is hidden.'

Actually, the villagers had no idea where such riches were stowed away. They would have welcomed some money themselves for the Town Hall needed painting, the Village

School a new roof, and the local fire-engine was old and decrepit.

Things, alas, did not improve. The robbers talked among themselves and soon all of them were saying that the villagers were really wealthy, with bags of money hidden away.

One day, four fierce men rode into the village and their leader announced: 'We are going to steal your children and, unless you pay a large ransom to get them back, you will

never see them again.' Then they picked up a boy and girl who were playing in the street, slung them across their horses' necks and galloped away. Their parents were distraught with worry.

The two children were terrified and screamed and struggled, and the robbers shut them in a dark wagon and threatened to kill them. They did not know what to do, but they were clever and observant children and, at dead of night, when the robbers were sleeping, they managed to tear a hole in the side of the wagon and squeeze through. Then, very stealthily, they crept out of the camp and made their way home.

It was a long walk, but as the sun was rising they saw their village below them, and knew that they were safe.

The robbers were furious when they found their captives had escaped. They leapt on their horses and rode swiftly back to recapture them.

This time the villagers were ready, and the robbers found themselves facing an angry mob of people armed with sticks and stones. They had not expected this and they turned and rode quickly back to their camp.

However, as they left, they shouted that they would soon be back to burn down the village and take all the children if the villagers' hoard of gold was not handed over.

This was no idle threat, and the villagers knew that the robbers would return in even greater numbers. A meeting of the Town

Council was called, to discuss what could be done.

'I have an idea,' said the Mayor. 'Not very far away from our own caves are some others, inhabited by several very large dragons. They have always been kind and helpful to us.' Everyone remembered the time that a tiny baby dragon had been rescued from a snow-drift and returned to his parents.

'Do you think,' the Mayor continued, 'that we could ask the dragons if they would come and live in our mountain caves? They are large, nearer to the road leading to the plain, and they are warmer too. We would willingly provide the dragons with fresh fruit and vegetables from our fields and gardens. The dragons will terrify the robbers, for they are very big. They can blow out quantities of hot smoke, and their eyes glow frighteningly in the darkness.'

So, a deputation visited the dragons and explained how afraid the villagers were that the robbers would return to destroy the

village and take all the children, and suggested to the dragons how they could help.

The dragons liked the idea that the villagers presented to them; they would gladly
move. Their present caves were too small and
they would love to frighten a band of wild,
wicked robbers. Also, they would quite enjoy
exploring the caves, and if they found any
treasure they would hand it over to the villagers because money was of no use to them.

So, the move was accomplished, and the
dragons settled happily into their new homes.
One day there was a great deal of noise and
shouting and the villagers saw a large band of
robbers approaching, armed with whips and
sticks.

'Take us to the caves at once,' they
shouted. 'Show us where your treasure is.'

The villagers pretended to be very scared,
and led the robbers up the path to the caves.

Then, suddenly, the dragons appeared,
blowing out vast quantities of hot smoke and
fire. The robbers drew back, terrified. The

smoke was so thick that they could not see where they were going. They stumbled back, falling over each other in their haste to get away. Soon there wasn't a robber to be seen – the villagers were safe!

The robbers never returned, as word soon got about that the mountain caves were full of terrible monsters.

The dragons settled down very happily.

Strange to say, they actually did discover two sacks of gold, which they handed over to the villagers. The Town Hall was repainted, the school had a new roof, and a very smart new fire-engine was purchased.

The dragons are still living there, to this day, and the village is very happy and peaceful once more.

The Town Hall Fire

It was a pleasant green meadow and lying in the sunshine were four large dragons. They had come down the mountain-side from the caves in which they lived. It was cold among the rocks and stunted trees, and the four dragons loved to feel the hot sun on their backs and take short dragon-naps, stretched out among the tall grasses and flowers. Not far away, across the meadow, they could see, in the little Chinese town, people hurrying to and fro, doing their shopping and talking to each other.

'Do you think it would be a good idea to pay a visit to the town and make friends with everyone?' said Dragon One.

'We are rather large,' said Dragon Two, 'and the streets are very narrow.'

'We might knock the houses down,' said

Dragon Three, 'and that would be terrible.'

'Let's fly over the town,' said Dragon Four, 'then we shan't do anyone any harm.'

So that evening the four dragons flew round the town. They made a tremendous noise with their huge wings and everyone was simply terrified. The children were called in from play, windows were closed, doors locked and barred, and the town became silent and dark.

'They are not very friendly folk,' Dragon One said, as he and his three friends finally came down in the Market Place, where they could just squeeze in.

'Let's visit all the little junks on the river,' said Dragon Two. 'I love being near water.'

The boat people, however, were just as alarmed as the townsfolk and refused to have anything to do with the dragons.

'Perhaps, if we took them some presents, they would see that we are really quite kind, helpful dragons, only wanting to be friendly,' suggested Dragon Three.

The Town Hall Fire

So the next day the dragons tried to think of something they could take to show how kind and gentle they really were.

Finally they arrived in the town with a basket of mushrooms, some little fish from the mountain stream and pigeon's eggs from nests near their caves. The townsfolk were still suspicious at first but eventually overcame their fear of the dragons and became quite friendly. So the four dragons decided that, as the weather was warm and the moon was full, they would treat everyone to a wonderful barbecue with all sorts of lovely dragon barbecue food.

The dragons, of course, had no difficulty in lighting huge charcoal fires with their hot breath.

Soon everyone was enjoying themselves and the dragons were delighted at the success of their party. In fact, they became so excited that they tossed hot charcoal about in a very light-hearted fashion, throwing pieces up into the air, catching them and chasing each

other round the smouldering fires. Then, suddenly, there was a cry from one of the townsfolk: 'The Town Hall is on fire!'

One of the dragons had obviously tossed up a piece of red-hot charcoal which had been caught by the wind and had landed on the wooden roof of the Town Hall.

There was a frightful to-do. The fire-engine was called and everyone rushed to the river and quickly formed a chain which passed buckets of water from person to person to throw on the burning building.

The four dragons helped, flying over the Town Hall carrying large buckets of water which they emptied on the smouldering roof.

At last the fire was put out but, alas, the Town Hall looked a sorry sight. Its roof had gone and its walls too, and there was thick ash everywhere.

The dragons felt very, very guilty indeed and flew sadly home, for they had been summoned to appear before the Mayor the next day.

'I'm sure we shall be expected to atone for our careless and bad behaviour,' said Dragon One.

'Well,' said Dragon Two, 'we can bring wood down from the forest around our caves to build a new roof and we are strong enough to put the wood in place.'

'Yes,' said Dragon Three. 'We can blow away all the dust and ashes and debris too.'

'Yes,' said Dragon Four, 'and don't forget the little hoard of money, the gold coins we have hidden in our cave. It is no use to us, but it would pay for new glass for the windows, paint to brighten up the building, and smart new furniture.'

The dragons worked really hard, fetching and carrying, putting large planks in place, erecting pillars and fixing window frames, and very soon a new Town Hall emerged,

even better and grander than the old one. Everyone was terribly pleased when at last it was all finished.

Then the new Town Hall had a wonderful official opening with guests invited from all the nearby villages.

Alas, there was no room for the four dragons in the new Town Hall. However, they watched the proceedings from the near-by meadow and were supplied with lots of

delightful food to eat. The Mayor gave them a special vote of thanks.

'Well,' murmured the four dragons, 'if we ever give another party we will provide cold food.' However, the dragons and the towns-folk remained great friends and the dragons felt really glad to know how welcome they always were.

Lam Ku, the Motherly Dragon

Lam Ku was a large, motherly dragon. In fact she was a little too motherly. Her dragon children had grown up and left home, but that did not mean that she didn't still hanker after a family of young dragons she could have around her to spoil, play with and feed. Unfortunately no one seemed to want to hand over their children to her care. When Lam Ku offered to take care of her neighbour's children, or dragon-sit at night, the neighbours refused. This made Lam Ku rather angry and unhappy, and she was determined to find some baby dragons she *could* look after.

It was no good staying where she was. She must travel the countryside where she might find some more amenable dragons who would be glad of her help with their children. She would have liked to have stolen some baby dragons, but she knew she would get into dreadful trouble if she did.

So, Lam Ku set off one fine day to see what she could find. Unfortunately, the first thing that happened was that she flew into a terrific storm. The thunder pealed round the mountains, rain and hail poured down, and she caught a nasty chill and had to find a warm cave to shelter in until she felt better.

Then she started off again, full of hope. But, no, fate was against her. Flying in the dark and not concentrating on what she was doing, she collided with a large tree, giving herself a nasty knock and bruising one of her wings. This meant another long wait while it healed.

She set off a third time but, alas, while swimming across a wide lake she got stung by a very unpleasant water-creature, and she felt so ill that she had to rest for a few days among some willow trees and rushes that grew by the lake-side.

Lam Ku, the Motherly Dragon

Oh dear, thought Lam Ku, am I never going to make any progress in my search? She had met very few other dragons on her journey, and although the ones she had stayed with had been, on the whole, kind, they were not over-welcoming and were certainly not prepared to hand over their children to her care.

She was beginning to get very weary of travelling, and yet she was determined to find what she wanted. One day, however, when she was flying above a little green valley, she saw below her a small Chinese village. She thought how pleasant it would be to have a rest among the kindly village folk, who were always very welcoming to visiting dragons if they behaved themselves. So, down she came in the Market Square and everyone greeted her in a very kind and friendly way, for Lam Ku had very nice manners. The children took rides on her back, and slid down her tail and fed her on delicious cakes, biscuits and fruit.

Then one of the village elders gave her a

tour of the village, pointing out all the important buildings. In fact, she was so kind and
understanding that Lam Ku told her all her
troubles – her longing to take care of young
baby dragons, her travels, and all the misfor-
tunes that had befallen her on the journey.

'My dear Lam Ku,' said the village elder.
'Have you never heard of the famous dragon
orphanage? It lies just beyond the village at
the foot of that tall mountain. There they take
care of all lost or abandoned young dragons
who have either wandered away from home or
have been neglected by their parents and are
in need of care and protection. I know that
their present superintendent is retiring, and
they are looking for someone to replace her.
Hurry off at once and apply for the job.'

Lam Ku was simply delighted, and it did
not take her long to reach the dragon orphanage at the foot of the mountain.

No one else had been found who wanted
the position of superintendent, so Lam Ku
applied immediately. Because she was so

motherly she was appointed at once. Lam Ku now found she had charge of twelve young dragons varying in age and size, which was just exactly what she had always wanted. It was not an easy job, some of the young dragons were very difficult and badly behaved, but this was just a challenge to Lam Ku and she simply loved her work.

The Dragon who Grew

The dragon community were very satisfied with the way in which she looked after the Home and took good care of all the young dragons. And if you are ever anywhere near this well-known dragon orphanage, pay it a visit. You will find Lam Ku is still in charge, as happy as a queen.